SONGS
OF
SISTER BIRD

By
ALEXSIS NEUMAN

Songs of Sister Bird   *Alexsis Neuman*

I guess this one's for me.

ISBN-13: 978-1535431156

All rights reserved ©

Songs of Sister Bird   *Alexsis Neuman*

Songs

Author's Note	1
Thoughtful.	2
DREAMER.	29
LOVER.	43
Beastly.	80
Reflection	117

Songs of Sister Bird   *Alexsis Neuman*

Author's Note

Hello All:

There are times when even the brightest of stars begin to glow dim. Still seen in the sky along with trillions of other stars, they feel a mere sparkle in comparison. Through times of struggle, it is important to remember—despite that your glow may occasionally seem to flitter into dullness, you are still a star.

Use your pain for profit. A soulful gain. Write it all out, setting aside the judgment or the false interpretation of flickering specks.

-Alexsis Neuman.

Nov. 7, 2013

1:00 PM

Thoughtful.

"A Mother's Strength"

If you were my daughter,

If you were my son,

I would pick you up and hold you close to me;

to remind you that you are protected and loved

Through your vulnerability I would remind you that you are strong.

Even if he has tried to dirty your mind and hands,

I would help you wipe them clean and grip them in my own.

I would brush your hair and hold the punching bag as you regained your strength.

I would do many things for you,

But I could not take away your nightmare.

I would help paint over it with new dreams;

with patience and care.

My daughter, my son, do not worry.

Be it your burden, I will bear.

March 25, 2016

12:07 PM

"All Apologies"

Saying "sorry" implies change.

You are not sorry,

you are the same.

When "sorry" comes to visit you,

with tears out of his eyes,

Meet him there with patience

for love is always kind.

And if "sorry" should outstay his welcome,

see him to the door.

A real "sorry" learns a lesson,

and is sorry no more.

March 22, 2016

11:32 PM

"A Happy Rain"

This rain

is my teardrops revisiting me.

To remind me why I left,

all at once.

To allow the sunlight to slowly evaporate me

back into the heavens.

April 26, 2015

1:03 AM

"Broken and Lovely"

I see you with your broken stare

And red knees

With your sore eyes

and strained voice.

You are still beautiful.

You see someone weak

& undesirable.

I see someone strong like iron,

surrounded by lilies.

Don't you know you're still lovely?

You can be broken, and still be lovely.

Feb. 22, 2016

8:02 PM

"An Ex"

Your hard-wired selfishness

Knows no bounds.

Oct. 6, 2014

"Misconception Conception"

She is much stronger than she realizes.

Mauled over by 3 weak excuses for human beings.

And courageously gave birth unto what resembled that evil and loved regardless.

She never understood how brave she was until I screamed it from the rooftops.

- I love you.

Feb. 9, 2016

7:02 PM

"You'll see"

I'll turn my pain into poetry.

It will be divine and misery-free.

And you'll try to be worth my resplendent lines

But I'll run out of ink when you cross my mind.

May 30, 2015

3:35 AM

"Free"

One day I will look down into the eyes of my child and I will not see you in their reflection.

Sept. 24, 2015

4:03 PM

"Notes to my Future Husband"

Someday I'll cry into your lap

about what he has done.

And you'll stroke my hair,

wishing you'd been there.

Though we were strangers at the time.

"Fair-Weather Friends"

No, I haven't the time for fair-weather friends.

With their help-me-now needs

& their quiet demands.

When they cry, I come running

With arms open wide;

But I'm left, feeling hopeless

No one by my side.

Such joy in those moments,

Tears we'd shed;

Ribcages shattered from

Laughter with nothing unsaid.

~Continued~

No secrets or anger,

All out in the open;

Serious-clowns,

& upset when we're joking.

Promises to help carry

Each other through;

You'd do for me, like I'd do for you.

Here I am carrying myself, yet again.

No one waiting for me out there at the end.

& I'd hoped it'd be different from the time we began—

But I haven't the time for a fair-weather friend.

2015

"Grace"

If grace is your only armor,

do not tarnish it with ill-will toward others

or rust it with pools of self-pity.

April 8, 2016

9:12 AM

"Another Note to My Future Husband"

"Are you worried you might run into him?"

Oh yes, definitely worried.

(But by worried I meant "hoping".)

I am much more worried that I won't.

May 30, 2015

4:53 AM

"Affirmations for a Terrible Wednesday"

I am important

Though today I feel forgotten.

I am intelligent

Though yesterday I was misinformed.

I am surviving

Though Friday I was barely here.

I am beautiful

Though I currently feel hideous.

Nov. 7, 2013

1:02 PM

"A Mother at Heart"

I will try to glue together

all your broken pieces

And I'll hold you til life pulls us apart.

You'll stretch me thin;

I'll say it is alright.

And I'll open my arms wide.

I'll cradle you,

Children you've become.

Like mothers do,

I will carry you.

June 9, 2015

11:48 AM

"Want."

I want to feel wanted again.

Warm.

Rosy.

Snuggled.

I want to feel funny again.

Abdominals hurting.

Cheeks flushed.

Smile, wide.

I want to feel dreamy again.

Hopeful.

Sexy.

Excited.

I want to be me again.

Prepared.

Confident.

Adored.

Nov. 7, 2013

12:52 PM

My dear silent companions:

One morning I will not have you serene, sitting beside me.

A content shadow that follows me through the house.

Radiating love, so pure.

And I will miss you so.

-All of my sweet pets.

Jan. 15, 2016

7:19 AM

"Empty Cup"

I must be my own rock before I am anyone else's.

I must be my own pillar, before I can stand strong enough for my children to lean upon.

I must calm my own sea, before I can let you swim in me.

Nov. 25, 2015

12:18 PM

"My Body"

I used to be so mad at

you for allowing purple

scars how i'd scrub you,

and you'd be red and

patchy.

how you could not seem to pick a shape and how you didn't

match what i saw how you were always hungry when I was

tired and didn't match societies standards.

Now, i love every hill and valley

and every dimpled

cheek.

"Wish"

I wish we had never met.

I wish we had never tried.

I am no better for having spent my time with you.

I am weaker. Broken.

I wish I had left sooner.

I wish no one knew, so I wouldn't have to hear their criticisms and answer their empty questions.

I wish you didn't exist.

So that when I left, I could not miss you.

I wish I hated you. It would be easier to go.

I wish they knew what really happened.

I wish their minds were open.

I wish I didn't care.

I wish I were wealthy, so that I could run off to an island far away.

I wish I could replace you.

I wish I could remove you from my memory bank.

~Continued~

I wish I could say you never mattered.

I wish I had never given you "me".

I wish my parents had kept us apart. I wish you could hear me when I speak.

I wish you would listen.

I wish I would've picked a different seat.

I wish I could've seen this coming.

I wish I hadn't been in denial this entire time.

I wish myself a brighter future.

I wish myself no more pain.

I wish myself a deserving husband.

I wish myself strength.

I wish you the best.

Just kidding.

I wish I were kidding.

(No, I don't.)

"Cement"

I am beautiful.

Maybe not conventionally…

But beauty, all the same.

I am too patient. It's okay to draw a line in the sand and then to seal it with cement.

I am loving and genuine.
Genuinely loving.

"A Warning"

What you do not choose to acknowledge is:

those sorts of secrets are not always forgivable.

You may not hurt someone on such a spiritual level & expect forgiveness.

"Street Pope"

I met a man who called himself a street-pope.

I knew they called him crazy.

He asked me for some change and I threw him what I could, even though I knew it wasn't going to anything good.

He wasn't much different than you or I-- Except he couldn't hide behind makeup, cars and lies. He's forced with his reality; we don't know why he's there.

I'm grateful for his existence. It reminds me why I'm here.

I saw a woman with a cart and 40 things she did not need, but what she wanted. It's nice to claim something when the world is a massive "nothing".

And you're alive, but dead.

I shouldn't assume she's hurting, but her face can't hide the pain. I see it as she pushes slowly, trying to cross the road in front of "real people". I hope she knows she matters.

She is someone's something.

Nov. 5, 2013

1:13 PM

"Just Leave Him Already"

I wouldn't give you up for anything.

Unless I learned it might make me cry less.

April 26, 2015

3:22 AM

"Comfort"

When I read you poetry,

You lay back and repeat your favorite lines.

May 29, 2016

8:29 PM

What a pretty flower…

I wonder how it grew?

I went and asked my mother to tell me what she knew.

She said it started out as a teeny, tiny seed.

Then she smiled and said that it reminded her of me.

Oh, poor little flower. It's wilting; now it's dead.

It makes so many questions pop inside my little head.

Mommy says that it grew old and that it had to go away;

I asked her why,

She began to cry

And said

We all do someday.

"Flowers of Age"

November 8, 2004

DREAMER.

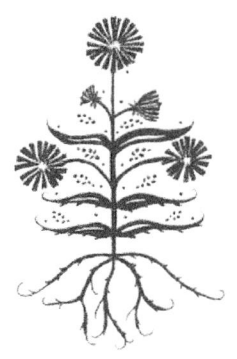

"Nightmare"

"I had a dream that I lived in a different place. The backyard extended into an almost woods-like area. We had a little glass flower house in the backyard buried in the brush.

And I don't know what I did, but you ended up back there. I forgot about you. You hurt me and I told you to leave. Suddenly, someone in my family had hurt me. I retreated to the glass-house on a sunny morning. I cried my eyes out and in the midst of my despair, I glanced out of the glass casing. There you were.

Vulnerable and upset. In your boxers and unaware of my prying eyes. Terrified that you had stayed so close to where I sleep, I carefully exited and got back to the front yard-- half a football field away.

I was so glad to be free of you. I just wanted to leave you back there. You made my heart skip. Half for the fact that I couldn't believe you didn't exit the vicinity, totally fearless that I'd see you again; and half for the fact that you were just as beautiful to me as before I knew you were such human-shit.

My eyes deceive me but I know better. Stay in the woods and don't you EVER come out."

Feb. 18, 2015

"Dream"

Did you dream again last night?

I really want to know.

Because I dreamed last night;

Of black snow and white waters.

Beehives & trapped birds

The usual, typically absurd.

Did you dream again last night?

Could you see her face?

When they leave us here, it is our secret meeting place.

Uncovered ocean floors, diamond skies.

I was flying low, near the borderline.

And heaven was so close

I could almost kiss the gates…

But I flew back down to avoid the taste.

I hope you dream tonight and that it's wonderful.

May it be everything you've wanted: calm and bountiful.

Dec. 29, 2013

5:57 PM

"Yearning"

I yearn for that familiar place

invented in my dreams.

It is so calm, so open.

So near waterfalls

and so very green.

No fear of being snuck up on,

no concern of when to leave.

Jan. 15, 2016

7:25 A

"And No One Came."

I dreamt of snow last night.

There was a cabin,

and a boardwalk surrounding

it in a great circle.

I was to walk it, searching.

They wanted me to find something

to help protect everyone.

Except, I don't know what I was looking for

And I was alone.

I helplessly dove through bouts of snow,

slowly losing hope as my eyes clouded over.

And no one came.

May 18, 2015

8:22 AM

"Weightless."

Though there is water in my eyes,

I see clearer than I ever did above it.

Bitsy, colorful friends drift with me as I delve deeper into their world.

My skin is as soft as the sand I glide past.

And as the sun leaves us, the darkness does not scare me.

I needed to know this place was real.

My hand tangled up in seaweed, I give it a hard tug to make sure this sensation is Actual.

How can I breathe?

Like magic. Like nothing.

I am a mermaid, and the fish are calling.

May 26, 2015

7:30 AM

"Sleep Sheep"

I have to think myself to sleep at night.

- you can keep your sheep

"Summer '07"

Let's lie here.

Unaware and unbothered by serpents.

I'll wear lace & you'll wear cotton,

and the stars will come into view.

We'll preach to them our spirit-plan &

hope the world grows quiet for a moment.

We'll smother the oxygen from the fire & be on our way.

Jan. 1, 2014

1:35 PM

"Dry".

I lay here, skin burning.

I wonder how it has not burned off yet.

I look, eyes slick with heat--

Liquid hot radiation off the earth I seep into.

I pray it comes soon.

Last chance, I blurringly round my eyes to

what lay ahead and behind me.

Nothingness.

Not a vulture in the sky.

I attempt to swallow--

a single drop of moisture tells me "no."

Crisping under the sun, I feel this must be

what hell is like. How are my thoughts still comprehensible?

A salted, pathetic tear drops from my closed left lid.

It is dry before it hits the dusty giant coffin called earth.

~Continued~

I sleep now.

My eyes open suddenly--

I hear muffled, sloshing sounds.

I move my heat stretched arms and know a new sensation under me. I am swimming!

How did this happen?

My weak elbows bend so that I may touch my face and I feel an ocean pouring from my eyes.

Skin peeling as I pat at my scorched cheeks, I cry and cry and cry some more

until I am practically drowning in these wonderful tears.

I ask God to shroud the overhead with clouds.

It seems he does not hear me.

Until… A fat, solitary cloud appears over me. And I float away.

My mind cooler, and my body carried.

Dec. 15, 2015

7:31 AM

"Depression"

It's like a hole filled with thick, black tar that goes on forever and circles back again.

And I have my arms, holding to the dirt I am sinking inside of—clutching to the rim for dear life.

The sweat from my red, tightly-shut fists creates a soft mud

allowing my arms to slide through it

Closer and closer I dip into the circle. And They all just stare. No one offers a hand, for they might fall into thick, black despair as well.

I cry, but it makes no difference.

A million thoughts race through my mind as I watch my last finger start to lose its grip-- almost broken in half from holding on so tight and for so long. It slips. As my eyes are glazed over with the dark goo, I watch Them all turn Their backs and walk away.

My lungs fill-- sticky with this mucus called "depression".

And I sink further…the light gets duller.

then there is no more sun.

~Continued~

I hear muffled water all around. Every scream I've never released pierces my ears. My two lungs damp as foam mattress soaked in honey and glue—pretending to breathe for me—but they lie.

It feels like the moment right before you'll give up and drown -- but the universe forces it into "repeat" for a thousand times. My soul, unaware of when the real Last Breath will come. No relief from this painful, awful, black sludge.

And then my finger pokes out and hits wind.

Glorious, glorious wind.

And I gather courage and stop kicking.

I float to the top-- blood from my nose, my ears deaf and my soul damaged.

I have crawled out.

I cling to the sides, swinging a leg over, beginning to roll to safety.

Then your boot comes down on my face.

"no happiness" is stamped into my forehead by the sole as it smacks into me over and over. My small fingers crushed, "let go or I shall cause you more pain."

And finally, I cannot bleed anymore.

~Continued~

So, I let go. And I sink, so deep.

100 feet…400 feet…900 feet…

My arms stop flailing. For no one is coming.

So, I gulp at the death-flavored-molasses

and I choke it down.

My unfamiliar body curls up, as I struggle to take a last breath. And the struggle for that breath continues for years.

And I pray for death to end it.

But death never comes.

Feb. 21, 2016

4:46 AM

"Rot"

I dreamt of death last night. What stuck out most were the last few moments of it. I'd sat down on a curb outside of a business complex and looked to my left. There was a dead puppy laying right side up. It had a milk belly, perfectly round. I stared at it because I knew no matter how devastatingly sad it was, there was no saving it.

Little ants were crawling across its neck. There was no life in that little body anymore, so there was no reason to be so miserable. The puppy wasn't going to feel the sun as it got hotter, only I was.

So, I got up, looked once more at it, and walked away.

As soon as I woke, the word "loyalty" kept ringing through my head.

June 30, 2015

9:11 AM

LOVER.

"J."

I could never love you.

You ask far too much.

The best that I can offer,

is an absent-minded touch.

Something to hold you over,

after all, I need it too.

Two distant hearts connecting,

flashing red as they bleed blue.

My heart is much too empty

I'd be poor if it meant wealth.

I could never, really love you.

For I do not love myself.

Sept. 16, 2015

6:03 PM

"I Wrote This in High School"

He told his son to help the helpless,
The ones who were like him.
The ones who could not help themselves,
The ones whose lives were grim.

She said to help the hopeless,
The ones who shared her fate;
The ones whose lives stayed loving
Even through their Dire Straits.

The boy will help the beaten, the broken
And the shamed. The ones who feel unworthy
To even speak His name.

God said to help thy neighbor,
And that's what you should do.
If you were left for helpless, my Neighbor,
Then you would need love to.

Feb. 28, 2007
7:51 PM

"Summer All Year Round"

Sometimes it's summer in your eyes.

And when I'm lost I like to lay there.

I miss your honey-suckled face

So, let's slip away from here.

There's a tire swing by the lake & it's where I go to forget now. I just soak in all the summer.

It's my favorite kind of sound.

I could listen to you play

All night long.

And if you got something to say, I'll be strong.

Because this wind can't blow me down,

Here it's summer all year long.

Jan. 24, 2015

"Goodbye"

Most of all, I will miss your ears

and the baby fuzz that line them;

the way your hair grows in perfect, brown tufts.

And the promise of what could have been, if you would have been.

Sept. 30, 2015

8:42 PM

"Tragic"

You are allowing a temporary tragedy to

permanently keep you,

And that's the real tragedy after all.

May 12, 2015

3:07 PM

"Almost"

I hoped so hard for someone like you…

and now that you're here, in the flesh

I never want to see you go.

What could have been,

shall never be.

I ran to you

And you ran from me.

Feb. 26, 2016

"Pranks"

I was so sure about you.

My gut had never let me down before.

Now I know, my heart is just as big of a prankster as my eyes.

May 30, 2015

3:38 AM

"So Far"

I could tell our story a thousand times,

a million ways,

and still not like the ending.

- do you remember

May 30, 2015

3:39 AM

"Pack Light"

I keep trying to pack you into my bag,

to carry you with me on my new journey.

But there is no room.

I remove essentials:

Self Love

Boundaries

Sacrifice

And in unpacking these things, I replace them with one: You.

But I find you are heavier than ten things.

You are marble dipped in metal.

You are a hot swing seat with no sprinklers in sight.

You are a brick wall with cracks so perfectly symmetrical that there is no room to catch footing.

I fall every time.

You are a burden.

Anchored beside me by love.

Unconditional love at that.

~Continued~

And though this is a telltale trait of pure love, it is also punishment in our chronology.

For the more I choose to lengthen the contract of nonexistent conditions, I let the rope rip through my hands-- rashing them until there is no more rope left to offer.

I am allowed conditions.

Even unconditional conditions.

My health is weakened and my melted brain is draining to one side of my thick skull.

When will I learn not to love so cripplingly?

March 8, 2016

9:07 PM

"I Regret You"

I know you think these tantrums will attract me.

Why else would you throw them?

Bring back my sunshine.

Your thunderstorms are repelling me.

I want to be your umbrella, shield you from the rain; but you'd rather stand in it, getting soaked in all your pain.

Nov. 25, 2015

"I don't know him."

Why are you asking me?

He's no different than the beggar-man outside who bothered me.

No, I don't know that smile. No, I don't know those hands. I don't know that scent, and I've never seen him dance.

He was never mine. & I was never his.

That was never my embrace & I wouldn't know his kiss. Stop saying you've seen love notes & pleas

To come to call;

He must be confused,

I don't know that boy at all. You know, we all are young, so perhaps he got it wrong? He better keeps to shadows, were his confused ass belongs.

Don't know his number, Or how he likes his beer. You should pass him to that young girl over there; Perhaps she enjoys games of the mind & love affairs. As for me, I wouldn't know— Those eyes don't look for me.

I never used to gaze at them & Hope that he loved me. He's never kissed my forehead and we've never shared a bed. We don't have a song; Could care less if he were dead.

~Continued~

I'm sorry to ask this of you, but please pass my note along. I wouldn't know that boy. Tell him to save his song. I'm just gonna keep it, wrap it up because I'm smart.

Never will they know…

He used to own my heart.

"I'm not skinny, but my soul is."

I'm no blonde, but it's a worthwhile exchange for what I've got in my heart can change what you think about brunettes with dark eyes and short lashes, thick hips and soft lips sweet for the tasting, pale souls of the feet, walking far from blue eyes wasting time waiting to figure out if my figure is worth your gaze; go figure every woman truly is beautiful naked and raw like my intellect, as if you could've matched it yet when all I've done is try to convince you of what you should've seen and known without issue and I may be curvaceous but my mind is bodacious, we could scream this together like two birds of a feather and weather that feather drift softly together into sleep, into your thoughts and wet dreams I'll creep and I'll be on your mind but I really don't mind, If you want, I'll come visit as a sea of doubt, I'll swim through but throw me a life coat that I can wrap around to keep me afloat as I row me a boat back to the land that these men walk about and worked so hard to steal who don't realize sexy isn't always blonde; but blonde can be sexy whenever it wants-- it might be, it's under the hair you see, inside the skull of that Beauty there are thoughts worth sharing more so than her limbs, and if you'd open your eyes you'd see past all of this-- this was fine but we're here now babe, I need to remind you of the progress we've made, so take all my scars and my crazy too, I may not be blonde: but I'll love you to the moon.

May 30, 2015

5:23 AM

"La Puente"

You just drove around the corner.

And I feel like I will never see you again.

It hurts very much.

I guess this is how it ends.

March 20, 2016

9:59 PM

"The EX."

I will not erase him from my photos,

as I cannot erase him from my memory.

And since that's all that is left,

I want you to see what I could see.

Dec. 1, 2015

12:03 PM

Isn't it cruel?

You tell them you've been hurt &

they listen to all the stories.

They tell you they can't fathom how

someone could be so careless with

such a delicate, rare flower.

Then they take your petals &

expect for you to stay in bloom.

"Well my mistakes are different?"

Just how is that?

How cruel.

Sept. 16, 2015

4:26 PM

"Him & He"

He wasn't my boyfriend

And that was okay.

He helped smooth over years of heartache, and pain.

I told Him I'd seen him.

He didn't care in the least.

He told me he'd turn out like He used to be; I just need wait and see.

I really thought Him wrong,

For when I looked into his eyes, I saw another life for me—one full of fun and surprise.

Of loyalty and affection, and intelligent conversation;

Not once did I assume, he would be one for alienation.

But He was right about him.

And He was right about Himself.

So now I sit alone,

Wondering if this is what it's all about…

Will they all be the same?

~Continued~

Though that's generic... is it true?
How could two different men I loved,
Be such awful fools?

"Chase Me Away"

If you loosen your grip,

I will slip through those calloused fingers faster than sand grains in a fit of wind.

Even if you gather up all of my pieces, I will never be that same pile of earth and dust again.

Forever changed.

Cover me in water to solidify where I stand. But your words will dry me out, and I will crumble once again.

8:03 AM

July 22, 2014

"Baby Father"

Thick, soft, tufts of dark brown hair intertwined between my fingers;

I tug tight and hold him near,

His lips bite down and linger.

The torture they survived was quite impressive

I must note;

I can't recall the taste now, though they had sent my mind afloat.

Lies ugly as sin but still, I wanted him.

And he rolled to look at me as if it weren't his bed

I was in.

If only I had known it was to be so fleeting,

I would've spent more time playing than sleeping…

May 6, 2015

"Sail"

I wanted for you to step back from the rubble;

to examine the fallen buildings

And far off explosions you had created.

For you to see the smoke steaming off of

the art work all around me.

To recognize the devastation and to see the hurt. but you shunned me. and you ran. It was what you were always best at. And my legs were tired of chasing you.

So, I watched as you built your boat and floated away, never looking back. I believe you caught my "I love you"

as it hit your sails and fell into your treasure chest.

Locked away with all of the other precious things

you decided you did not need anymore.

Feb. 26, 2016

11:46 PM

"Love Lost"

Honeyed words and familiar scents;

His best offerings.

A sleeve where my heart usually lay;

His arm remains bare.

Ballooned up ideas and marvelous dreams;

My feet on the ground, walking a straight line.

A world all our own, that even we might not inhabit much longer.

Soft hands & nuzzled noses, so comfortable & safe.

That mellifluous baritone, pulling at my invisible strings…

How does it know to do that, even when I've been at sea this long?

No desire to solve the mystery; Only a longing to explore. We'll carve our dreams in trees & count the clouds up high once more. And I'll wake to find myself watching those puffs glide by alone;

I'll gently pull myself aside & move my life along.

"Eternally"

I want for you to rise up, creating a world beneath your feet. To love yourself so much that my love is whipped cream to your sweat cocoa.

I want for you to climb so high that the air becomes thin; to meet you with a tank of oxygen.

I want for you to be so sure and decisive that it is proven you want me. Not that you need me.

And in that, we will be happy eternally.

Sept. 30, 2015

6:03 PM

"Don't do it"

I whispered to myself

as he leaned closer and closer into me.

Because if you do, I'll have to pretend I hated it.

"Half of a Man"

If you drop them once more, I cannot hand them back.

These keys are your way out, think of it like that.

You show half of your face, and it's the beautiful side.

The one he fell for, the one full of pride.

You have another, it's beautiful too;

one he does not know

and it is shining-on through.

If he's worthy of you, he'll understand.

If not, stop presenting you as a whole for half a man.

May 30, 2015

3:42 AM

"Crawl"

I'd say I was sorry,

but that'd be a lie.

Which I am no good at

So, I won't even try.

I needed my peace,

I craved my pride

So, for him I did buckle

for him I did die.

No, it wasn't appreciated

Or remembered at all--

but I just had to try.

Back to him I will crawl.

May 30, 2015

"Perfect"

He said he wanted perfect

and there I stood

But he did everything

to prove he was no good

He beat me til

I resembled raw meat.

My mind was defeated

and my muscles weak

I cried and begged and pled

he would change.

I led by example

every. single. day.

But it wasn't enough

no, it never truly was.

Over time I was broken,

though I'd prayed to be tough.

~Continued~

He let others audition

He lied to my face

Even when I gave in

And I'd lost all my grace;

Jailbroken his phone,

lies carefully covered

he'd learned how to lie

and be fake to his mother.

I shouldn't be shocked

and I guess that I'm not

I'd just hoped one day

He might miss me… a lot.

"Lady Bird"

Please God grant me today with this love;

allow it to be strong through the evening.

Don't know what I'll do without this love;

and this new, hollowed out, feeling.

My guardian angel, my almost first born;

watches my tears from Heaven & my heart as it's torn.

Every birthday since 7, every breakup and grade;

paws crossed, patiently waiting on the soft bed I've made.

Calm green eyes,

delicate, velvet ears.

This has been my true love all these years.

Please don't leave me now,

when I need you the most

My teacher, my child, my guardian ghost.

They won't understand, not in full

there is no way.

~Continued~

Not until Heaven when they see us someday then maybe they'll get it

the bond that we have made.

Pure, & real, & honest, & safe.

I'll love you forever,

no matter where you go;

I'll meet you there soon,

for my time here is short.

I'll talk to you often, as if you were here;

I'll wish I could hold you, so close and so near.

I will love you forever, until your last day.

And I'll love you until we're together someday.

Sorry I'm such an asshole,

-I miss you.

May 6, 2015

9:23 PM

"Sublime."

I asked her if she missed him.

A question I knew the answer to.

With her light she smiled and said, "Of course. But I will see him again."

Though I believed her, a part of me still wondered…

You may KNOW this at your core, but does your heart not break with each passing

anniversary? Birth, death and marriage?

Do your eyes not water when you hear his voice on the radio?

Do your lips not tremble at the memory of the last kiss you two had shared?

Or is it that you visit him so often in your dreams

that you have not had to miss him other than when your eyes are open?

Her smile faded then.

I could see her remember his scent.

~Continued~

His warmth.

Every crease in his face. Every fight.

All of her devotion.

Knowing her True Love, was now scattered in the ocean.

And much like her healing heart, his spirit surfs upon the wave.

His may have been a short journey,

but look at all the love he gave.

May 19, 2016

12:40 AM

"Promises from the Ex"

"I hate that I hurt you"

"That's not me anymore"

But when I wrap my arms around you for comfort, you recoil in disgust.

Turning back into the snake I thought a grizzly bear.

"I am a different man now"

"I just feel hurt"

You forget I have 7 years of pain behind me;

I am a rabbit, a mouse, a fish.

Quick, small, timid

And now, swimming free. Do not catch me with your net. Swim beside me in through these dark waters until we find crystal-clear oceans. Do not scream that there are waves, when you are the only one flailing away in these once calm waters.

April 25, 2016

8:15 PM

"Speak to me as you spoke before"

Love me as you always swore

Love me, Dear, forevermore

and breathe me sweetness, into my core.

Tell me the things you won't tell her

Let me feel you care for sure

Lend a hand into my heart

And keep it safe from Evil's part.

Let me see into your soul,

past your half, into your Whole

Kiss me sweetly

Hold me tight

And I will fear

No dark, nor night.

Aug. 18, 2007

9:50 PM

Beastly.

She described it as "insidious"

and I'm afraid, that's true.

A never ending circle

of dark thoughts inside of you.

- depression

Sept. 16, 2015

5:58 PM

"Strive Force Cry"

I can't get there fast enough.

Strive and strive and strive and strive.

It's taking too long…

Persevere and pray and pray and persevere.

Can anyone come with me? I'm scared to go in there alone.

Force and force and force and fall.

I need help climbing back out…

but there is no help to call to.

Cry and cry and cry and sleep.

Nov. 7, 2013

12:53 PM

"What He Has to Offer"

And what have you to offer me?

Words of kindness? Words of falsity?

Certainly not words of fairness and honesty?

Do you assume that what's between your legs will hold my heart up?

Do you know your worth?

April 20, 2015

3:50 AM

"When Pretty Girls Cry"

She looked at me with disdain and I snapped back,

"And so what if he has touched you? Do not let him win.

You are just as perfect as BEFORE. Mourn if you must.

But you are still as delicate, as soft, as worthy and amazing

as any other brilliant woman."

She cried again but this time I believe it was because she knew a new lightness in her

soul.

I hate when pretty girls cry.

Jan. 15, 2016

1:50 PM

"An unrequited love."

I bathed him in compliments about his skin so fair.

I rub his aching back and gently stroke his hair.

I watch him run to others, glancing at my saddening face.

Searching for "a someone" to fill his heart's empty space.

Rejected time after hour by the man I thought I loved;

Clearly, I am not enough, his spell I must fall out of.

As I hear the bells ring with the song of holy togetherness,

And I watch the Bride depart with my Groom in tender-bliss.

The glow she wore burned in my mind—the one I was to wear.

And she stole all my happiness

To have

To hold

To share.

To see him walking lonely as my feelings pushed to shove— It's a feeling worse than death.

April 30, 2007

"No One Left"

If you truly missed these mothering arms so much

You would not point a sticky, punch-stained finger at my wounded eyes and scream, "You did this"

Yes.

I did.

But what I have done, all I have done, only happened with 8 years of abuse behind them.

I committed one act of selfishness to counter your 800 lies.

So that I would not drown to death in my self-sorrow.

I am not abandoning you.

I am freeing you.

What?

Is it not fun anymore when there is no one left to disappoint?

"At Best"

I am a Woman.

A strong-willed, tender hearted, pure-soul of a human.

And the best you'll do is with a young, blind fool; or a woman-in-training whom is so sure but so unaware of her untapped womanly potential.

Oct. 6, 2015

8:47 AM

"Learning Alone Time"

Does the mundane scare you?

Like it scares me?

I know I've done fine with complacency.

I won't wander past my walls,

I'll be fine where I am.

I just worry that they'll leave me

& I'll be alone again.

July 6, 2015

3:41 AM

"Misery's Love-Child"

There are only dark clouds here.

I must have believed too hard. Burst the bubble of hope I had been trapped inside of for so long.

I am misery's love-child.

The map I had drawn out leads to nowhere;

suddenly written backwards and crumbling at the corners.

I was supposed to have a partner on this journey…

but he slipped into the quicksand.

I tried to save him.

He did not want to be saved. He left me all alone out here; with the snakes and the beetles. I'd leave me too, except, I'm attached to this body.

I don't like these tiny, lidless, leering eyes…

I am not selfish enough to leave so soon.

I know my pain will settle upon you,

and those spectral pupils will haunt you, too.

Nov. 6, 2013

4:10 PM

"Aging Youth"

Again, I mold my thoughts like bread.

These spinning wheels inside my head.

Sleepless, over-worked and tired

Can't catch a dream, even if I tried.

Pencil tip was broken

So I sharpened up the knives

And as he smiled, he scared me

With those piercing emerald-eyes.

Royal mention to my Mother; get her safely out of town.

Rush me to the sacred pond and drown me with a frown.

Freckled-wing upon the window,

Brush me off til dawn. I would join you all for dinner,

But you're sure to hear me yawn.

Fold your napkins neat like logic,

Bare in mind the only truth;

Pour me another tonic

And leave my aging youth.

"2675 Days"

What have I learned about you in 2675 days?

That you like to make assumptions.
That I am not a priority, even at my worthiest.
The less I speak, the more I am desired.
The more I express, the more I am ignored.

I am too loud, too proud and too valuable to be left to collect dust.

"And He is Love"

I did not hand you the needle to sew these two lips tight.

I was afraid of this…

The judgment that might come from sharing what I wanted to experience with what I had hoped so dearly would be a kind world.

You were kind. Because you were gaining something too. But now that you have ran your race, I see that angry growl spreading from the back of your mind.

I see it growing blacker and blacker with envy. That I might be yours for one moment. One powerful, meaningless moment. And that it might be nice. Very nice. But that I would return to where I came, happier and solid. I can smell you stewing.

Your hatred must contain itself. It will not win me over. I belong to another. Someone with the patience of a god. Someone that allowed me to be free. That built me a castle made of gold and set the draw-bridge down, allowing me to come and go as I please. And he is Love.

And if you think I would ever let that go in a million of God's years, you would be insane.

"Goodnight"

My head was pounding,

nose dripping.

Why aren't I ready for this?

I can't think straight.

My knees are buckling as I lay down.

I don't want to lay any longer.

I want to run.

So I run to you.

And miraculously, you are awake.

Sitting in the dark, dazed.

I crawl to you.

You hold me as long as I need.

And my headache disappears.

And I swallow my fear-filed snot.

And you kiss my burning cheek.

And I feel a little stronger

Jan. 4, 2016

4:02 AM

"Stale"

It's not a pressing matter for him anymore.

Though it bogs me each day, it doesn't seem to weigh his thoughts down

in the least.

My trust, suspended in midair, shaking like a novice trapeze artist.

I shall pay for your mistakes again, to finally find the truth in all of this.

Maybe then you'll realize that I knew all along.

And there will be no denying it.

Dear Girl Who Came After:

I knew you'd be a December fling.

I knew he couldn't love you. I knew he lied through sparkling teeth and made you feel alive. I know your heart skipped three beats as he promised you the world.

And I know the pain is excruciating--

Of that, you can be sure.

And I know you think I condensed here, but I adamantly oppose. For you see, I was a budding flower that he loved into a rose.

And he ripped me from my soil, simply to see where the roots had drawn. And once he saw how long they were, he left me there to mourn. He picked another flower, a daisy   far away. Unaware that I'd replanted myself & began to grown again.

I stand tall here in the sun now,

and though his shadow pass--

I believe you will grow stronger too, this pain isn't meant to last. Once he has plucked the garden clean & word gets

round that he's a chore, you'll see why I wrote this letter.

Love,

The Woman Who Came Before

"Love is Not Obsession"

No one could love me for long.

Because there will always be someone more worthy of obsessing over.

July 30, 2015

5:45 AM

"Weekends."

Weekends

are

for

funerals

And for catching up on sleep.

April 18, 2015

6:55 AM

"Good idea."

Instead of letting men grow,

let's replace the soil with cement and see how far they go.

Good idea.

Let's block all the sunlight,

shading me from that glow,

so, all my roots can't soak it in and

I become a seed once more.

Good idea.

Step on me and watch me bounce like an accordion.

Swaying in the wind,

pollinating others' gardens

because I've had no room to spread my own.

Good idea.

What should've been a mighty rose,

is now an UNcracked seed. If you had

watered me and moved aside, we could be at peace.

"Realization"

White

cream

custom.

Toppers

pearls

lace.

Promises on paper…

That day will not come.

Watered eyes

hopeful faces

Delicate flowers,

rings and doves

The long walk, long wait, hold our breath and dance…

That day will not come.

Union in the grass, sun high in the sky

Kids running, giggling, playing…

Through the door in strong arms

That day will not come.

"I Will Not Blink"

Do not tell me that I do not know Darkness.

He has stared me dead-on while my family suffered at his hands; mocked me as I rocked back & forth, needing to forget. He is a thief and I am forever on my guard.

He is the devil and I hide behind God.

He has threatened to take what makes my life Real. I bravely shouted at him that I would go in their place. I know my job here; and for the prize I give away, it is a worthwhile task indeed.

I was chosen for a reason and I do not take it lightly. I take pride but I take no boastful stance. It is hard. It is painful. But I swore I would do my best.

So here I am, toe to toe with Darkness again.

I will not blink

I will not conjure a thought.

I will not lose this war with such a weak, unloved, uncreated, ugly demon.

I will not blink.

"We Were Each a Goddess"

Every time I think I miss you,

I look to her and see the pain

you've caused out of your own selfish wants -- not needs.

Each one of us has a mind,

a humongous, forgiving heart,

fiery passion,

a uniqueness unlike any other.

& patience.

Each of us was not like the other.

And each of us was beautiful for it.

And it was never enough for a

demanding, attention-seeker like yourself.

May 12, 2015

3:09 PM

"Notes to my Future Husband…87"

I want to call you over.

I'm scared of the dark.

Skin on skin,

your skin in my skin

Our spirits gently wrestling; bodies singing like a lark

I've been flying around free

Your blessing under me

Trust to trust

Your must versus my lust.

I want to taste all 32 flavors

But the sweetest I've tasted is the one Cuervo-wasted

Kiss these lips good bye. Cigarette on tongue is cancer:

So am I.

Those are the wrong lips. Don't look me in my eyes. Only one to ever get to me, and he never kept me high.

April 3, 2016

4:16 AM

"I worry I am not pretty enough for him."

His words hit my exterior, and fall fast, letting gravity do their job as they cannon toward the floor

un-absorbed.

He says I am, and he is tired of telling me.

Sir, you would not have to tell me over and over if I knew it to be truth. If it burdens you to tell me something so sweet and pure and raw

If it annoys you, pains you, drives you mad:

You should not tell me anything except "goodbye".

Yes, I shall lay in a heap.

I shall power through tears and crumble at our could-haves. But I should be able to shrivel and prune at my will.

And resurface a new woman, without you calling still.

April 25, 2016

8:10 PM

"Rush"

You were a protective fence.

I planted flowers.

They would blossom,

And you would tell them to die.

I hopped out, and you surrounded me again.

I admired your engravings.

I planted more flowers.

You spit on them with black tar.

You are like a tar-filled pillow, covering my face, over and over.

April 20, 2016

2:29 PM

"Listen"

I will tell you how a good woman cheats.

When a good woman has done all of the chores;
Laundry, dishes and something more—
Dealt with his past as a neglected child,
Lonely nights and school-days wild
When she's learned of his violence and poor
Reputation & she's nurtured his growth toward

A man despite his lack of motivation;
And she's taught him to love on a spiritual level
And how to be grateful no matter the weather;
When she's spoken to him about God & her dreams;
When she's cried in his arms lost to his selfish disease;
And she's coward down timidly at the strike of his hand,

Still craving so deeply that wedding band;
And she's spent all her logic on him and his ways;
And he speaks ill of her to his mother, to her dismay;
And she's done all his homework so that he might pass,
And she's supported his poor choices and guided him best. When she's gently prodded him into a man—yet all of her

~Continued~

efforts Fall from his plan. And no matter her tears, he still sleeps Around, and his words are empty and he's stolen her crown. Her world is a mess, her investment irritated, Her cheeks burn with embarrassment at all the time wasted—

When she's realized her worth through dumb defeats,

That is when a good woman cheats.

April 27, 2015

3:29 PM

"They"

My scent does not stick out here.

I'll just attach myself to the mulch.

I'll just blend here.

I'll just be here.

They aren't mean. They aren't expectant.
They listen when I cry. They let me get it all out.

I won't want to talk when We become warm.

I'll want to be alone again.

Leave me here to blend.

Nov. 6, 2013

"Better than Before"

Why aren't I stronger yet?

Where is the strength I prayed for?

I fell out of bed.

I pushed through the day.

Where is the strength I heard you whisper for me?

I need it terribly.

I can't go on much longer, waiting for support.

I don't want to cry as soon as I crack open my eyes.

I don't want to ache when I dress myself.

These chores aren't simply mindless anymore.

I'm breaking into pieces, like these shattered porcelain plates.

Please, before I am old. I want to be better than before this happened.

Nov. 7, 2013

12:41 PM

What a miraculous feeling it is

when you have prayed for Death

and he does not come for you.

- Hang on please.

Feb. 9, 2016

6:50 PM

"Lies I Tell Myself"

Hopeless and empty and out on her own.

These aren't wife-like qualities.

Try, except you've tried too hard. Too long.

Who wants a broad like her anyway?

Foolish, romantic and destined for the basic.

Shouldn't be here.

Why does she speak when no one wants to hear her mouth?

These ideas are far from original.

She is centuries from special.

April 20, 2015

3:53 AM

"Idle Hands"

Your hands are very busy. Keep them that way.

Idle hands are not your worry.

My hands should be on a piano,

on a warm chest,

Clutching a waning pencil,

coddling a small version of myself.

But instead, my hands are shaking, holding up my heavy head.

They have to stay there, to hold it up.

Who else is supposed to do it?

Everyone else's hands have work.

This IS my work.

Nov. 6, 2013

3:52 PM

"Cherry"

I too, have gazed upon her naked body.

The difference is: I know how to navigate it.

Oct. 1, 2015

12:57 PM

"Notes to my Future Husband…43"

The sheets will swallow you,

As I shall swallow you.

But you must be patient…

"Under the Garden Wall"

He used every reason to rest a hand on me gently.

Any excuse, and he would leave it there--

touching for only moments.

I am careful not to light the kerosene that spills from his lips.

Though I wonder if these hands are as soft as they look plucking the strings of his weathered guitar.

11:28 AM

"D.M.H."

I remember he wanted the lights on,
And I shook my head.
He looked disappointed but did what I said.
CLICK
The lighting was still too honest in here.
I stared at him, a silent "no"
And CLICK, he crawled in slow.

And I had to check my pulse to make sure I was still alive.
He slowly helped me reanimate the dead spirit inside.

My first image of that moment was my hand face up
On his pillow; without me saying anything, he CLICK
Wound like a willow.
Surrounding all of me, like ten men all at once--
It would've lasted 30 nights, but Daylight came for us

May 7, 2015
12:22 PM

Reflection

I try to write from my real life, to reach deep within and to authentically recapture my true emotions at that moment in time. I share these thoughts for those who might resonate.

To every person who took the time to read over my passages, regardless of your views and beliefs—thank you.

My wish is for every person to know self-satisfaction, self-love and respect for themselves as well as for every living being, plant and creature.

Thank you for your time,

A. Neuman

Songs of Sister Bird *Alexsis Neuman*

Made in the USA
Las Vegas, NV
21 November 2020